The Walls of Thebes

Other Poetry by David R. Slavitt

Suits for the Dead
The Carnivore
Day Sailing
The Eclogues of Virgil
Child's Play
The Eclogues and the Georgics of Virgil
Vital Signs: New and Selected Poems
Rounding the Horn
Dozens
Big Nose
The Elegies to Delia of Albius Tibullus

The Walls of Thebes

Poems by David R. Slavitt

Louisiana State University Press
Baton Rouge and London
1986

Designer: Christopher Wilcox
Typeface: Palatino
Typesetter: G&S Typesetters, Inc.
Printer: Thomson-Shore, Inc.
Binder: John Dekker & Sons, Inc.

Some of these poems have appeared in *Boulevard, Chelsea, Light Year '84* (Bits Press, Cleveland, Ohio), *Poetry Northwest, Prairie Schooner,* and *Southern Poetry Review.*

The author expresses thanks to George Garrett and to Henry Taylor for their kindness and their help in the preparation and ordering of the manuscript of this book.

Publication of this book has been supported by a grant from the National Endowment for the Arts in Washington, D.C., a federal agency.

Library of Congress Cataloging in Publication Data

Slavitt, David R., 1935–
    The walls of Thebes.

    I. Title.
PS3569.L3W3   1986   811'.54   85-23845
ISBN 0-8071-1306-9
ISBN 0-8071-1307-7 (pbk.)

In memory of my mother

Contents

The Walls of Thebes

Visions

A flight of birds, hundreds, a cloud of them, wheeling,
enlivening the springtime Maryland air;
or, on the way to Boston, just past Norwalk,
those half dozen hot-air balloons in flotilla,
a progress of dowager queens across the sky;
or, once in Wyoming, that glimpse to the side of the road
of a pair of antelope blurring away through a meadow . . .
Snapshots. Gifts. Even to juxtapose
and catalog them thus is wrong. My breath
caught; I was caught up; I was held; I held
the wheel steady driving through the moment
that blessed hour. There ought to be halos:
smiles make do but fade. It all fades
away, or nearly all. Still, I can remember
enough to wonder how I could just drive past
those rare moments. What kind of brute could?
But it isn't such hoarded visions that can redeem us
so much as the hope that their like may happen again.

Herz-Werk

The eyes and ears, let us say, bite, and the brain
digests, chewing the cud, but the heart absorbs:

this is the system by which the soul is nourished
and it builds—as fat and muscle accrete—wisdom.

Comes then like some tv-fitness bozo
with a program of strenuous calisthenics, Rilke!

Do I go too far? Well, make him a music master
and his Herz-Werk a kind of piano practice,

three against two, upon the psyche's grand
instrument, exercises of just feeling.

The trick is sitting there upon the bench
and hearing the notes sound, first in the head,

then in the air, the hands still in the lap.
Stillness has its voice. One must learn to hear it.

Let it sing; it is not a trick, or rather
the trick is for it not to be a trick.

Now get up from the piano and walk away
as if the music still held you together,

as if all pianos did not have to fight
the terrible habit of their vibrating strings

to die. The sostenuto pedal, the trills,
the tricks of the repertoire are all undone.

A note dies in the air and then the next.
Not even cadenzas' boisterous runs

can fill the maw of the hall. Lively applause
cushions but cannot hold the fading strain.

Later, we may recall a phrase as it blurs
to its extinction. The stillness afterwards

is not like the stillness that came before
but bloodier, and the blood has dried. It's rare

and delicate nourishment, but on such morsels
Rilke's finicky inner beast depends.

Wading

The tongue tip of the cold wave
licks your toes—it's great fun
to toy like this with so huge a beast,
apparently tame and lying supine
beneath a Crayola sun. You dare
a step further and maybe another,
and feel the cold more at the ankles
and calves now than the feet, numb
already or somehow hardened to
the bracing water. You also notice
the weight of the waves as they come ashore
and their gentle tug receding. A dog
would tussle thus at a rawhide bone,
a puppy that hadn't any idea
of its size or strength, horsing around.
The sparkle, the salt, the bluish green
sluicing invites, taunts you to take
its challenge and a step further
and deeper into the bright water,
and then the bottom falls abruptly
away just when you need it, when
a larger than average breaker gives you
a not so gentle cuff, and you fall
and feel the tug of the undertow
taking hold not quite in earnest
but giving you something to figure from
as you calculate its power and shudder
with a chill of fear as you clamber back
up the steep slope to the smooth
sand, a terry towel, and safety.

Months later and hundreds of miles
away from the moment, it still hangs
like a question mark, a wave about to
break and engulf the declarative
sense you thought your life was making.
The unpredictable currents—of passion,
disease, or fortune—that swirl harmless
about your ankles could at the next
innocent step bowl you over.

But you're no fool and have understood
that those are among the risks of the game.
Still, that feeling of being lifted
up and carried away by some
huge and indifferent power, that birds
and fish in the great currents of air
and water know in their fragile bones,
murmurs into the inner ear's
delicate balances and you
go giddy, knocked one way by fear
and pulled back by the undertow's
embrace that waits like a patient lover.

The Shadow

What boy has never envied Lamont Cranston,
invisible, able to fight for truth and justice,
defend his country, or slip unseen—and naked,
of course—into the girls' shower at school?
It isn't the trick we imagined but an art,
severe in its discipline, arduous (most of them are).

The limpid waterdrop, the rarefied
upper air, the even more abstract
refinements of science—radar or sonar—
betray nothing; this is the heart of the matter,
that knack of selflessness, the purity
of attention that never refracts, never reflects.

You see, or don't, the perfectly clear pane
in shop windows. They curve, disappear, tempting
the not-so-innocent passerby to suppose
he might reach out to scoop up a quick handful
of gold and gems. That appetite for riches
is what the illusion is likely to kindle. The real

abnegation of crystal—if only the ball
were perfect, we couldn't see it at all, and the gypsy
might yet peer into the future's maw—
sets the impossible standard of refinement
I know enough now only to dream of:
to sneak into that school shower, to see

with neither lust's reflection nor sentiment's
refraction those girls' young bodies and as clearly
their lives and deaths—as Dr. Chekhov might,
or angels were they to eavesdrop on their giggles.
I have held my breath so to listen
to a brook's faint purl I thought I'd imagined

but couldn't imagine where. All of us know
what evil lurks in the hearts of men. What's harder
is what is good and unremarkable
except to the gazing eye, flawless, selfless
as that glass, air, water. Obtuse, opaque,
The Shadow got it wrong, knew nothing at all.

5

Eye Test

Children say they see individual leaves
but they lie or at least blur the truth a little,
conforming to what they think we want to hear

or what they can bear themselves to believe or doubt.
And yet we think them honest witnesses,
for the leaves, indeed, are there, each with its own

stem on the branch just as the tree in the child's
clear eye, focused on exactly,
has its accountable countable leaves too.

Older, our senses yield postimpressionist
riches, the eyes' failure a triumph of truth:
soft as nursery toys the plush trees

swim in my yard, float on tides of air,
and ride the floods and ebbs of light, their masts
ashimmer in heat upon the continuo

ripple below. What daggers children look,
slicing their world so fine . . . Or make them nails
with which they tack each fleeting object still,

ignoring its wriggle to mount it, nicely dead,
in its box—or so one might fear, but, no,
the nails rust, ravel, seem to bear fur,

relax and blur into bloom so that details,
crucified, rise again, and their dry bones
knit, flex into motion, and dance in a light

that dances with them. Weathered myself, I see
through wet lenses my block a glitter of jewels
and familiar streets strung with glorias, halos,

as simple vision gives way to the visionary.
Below that big black E, the chart on the wall
turns into nonsense Belshazzar paid so richly

to have explained, though a child could read it directly:
you have been weighed and found wanting (Again?);
and the end is near. One learns to say Amen.

Bloody Murder

Beauty and truth may dally together,
but when it comes time to pop the question,
it's ugliness that settles in
to take the vows with truth for the long
haul, the enduring and faithful companion.
The difficult lesson we all must study
is how to be children of such a marriage
and honor what we cannot love.

After the burglar bludgeoned my mother
to death with a bathroom scale and a large
bottle of Listerine, the police
recommended Ronny Reliable's
Cleaning Service—one of a growing
number of firms that make it their business
to clean up after messy murders,
suicides, and other disasters.

They have the solvents and strong stomachs
for such work. I still wonder
who would choose that kind of employment
or what the men who performed this awful
and intimate task looked like. We only
spoke on the phone; detectives let them
in; and the charge showed up on my next
Mastercard bill. But I know they were there.

The chemical smell hung in the air
of the empty house for nearly a month,
proving they'd been there and done the job,
which is to say that the other unthinkable
thing had happened first. Excess,
whether of pleasure or pain, beggars
belief so that lovers and mourners rub
their eyes in similar ways, trying
to take in the thought along with the image.

One needs both. On the KLH
radio my mother kept on
top of the bureau, there was a white

electric cord the assiduous workers
missed with its evidence a doubting
Thomas needs or dares, to challenge
nerve and love, the reliquary
stain of what had been done and undone.

It wasn't a bullion cube, would not
reconstitute in heat and water,
but there it was, to be faced, the mark
of faceless functionaries, furies,
or Ronny Reliable's Cleaning Service.
Jesus knew how it was—and wasn't—
a comfort to tell his stunned disciples:
this is my body, this is my blood.

The Last Dalmatian

1

Imagine, as I often do,
a woman, old and sick in her whitewashed
hovel overlooking the Adriatic.
The year is maybe 1902.
Once as a girl, she learned
words for *goat, fish, water, sky*
in her mother's mother-tongue,
what everyone in the village spoke—
but the village dwindled away, and the countryside
took up whatever Serb or Croat
dialect was then in use among
the townspeople. Dalmatian shrank to a joke,
the lyrics to songs, a proverb about the weather.
Curses and dirty words
survived a while longer.
But she was the last, this woman, really to speak
the language. No academician came
with tape recorder or even a notebook
to make a career by taking down
whatever she mumbled as she turned the air
briefly Dalmatian again,
losing each day a little more weight and spirit
until she was gone, her mouth a gaping
hole in the universe, or universal O
we all recognize as the mother-tongue
of pain and woe.

2

Each of us has suffered losses, each
has felt the terrible wrench of earth
shrinking beneath his feet.
There's less and less room to stand.
Gone are such exotic treasures
that once were the simple parts of speech.
What we mourn is not the body
but all those unmade sentences, rich
in history and desire, none

ever to be uttered now. The lexicon
and grammar have disappeared,
and Alexandria's library is burned.
If only I'd studied more and learned
by heart some of the basic texts. They're gone,
and I am the ignorant victim of my own
sloth. Grief and shame choke the random
smatterings I remember of English or Yiddish.
I am a parrot, can say, "Hello, hello,"
and utter at inappropriate moments a few other
simple phrases, telling all I know.

Magma

To the dumpy tenor and fat soprano
we close our eyes, trusting our ears
for the transports of their duet's passion—
a primitive habit, that lids' closing
out such extraneous detail
to allow an inner order the triumph
it needs sometimes. Or is it more
to seal in the rare instant,
the nerves on fire, the marrow molten,
able to take an impression, cool,
and then hold it, not forever
but until the forge or rust's slower
fire shall nibble it blank again?
Fresco is like that, or fresh-poured
concrete, tempting to naughty boys
who want to proclaim their names and loves
enduringly. They get it wrong,
for hardness is never hard enough
to endure through that eternity
they think they imagine. What counts more
is how the softness happens, the heated
and glowing moment when rock and metal
behave like water. And human hearts
can likewise writhe, free for a moment
to pour, dance on the anvil, marry
the mold, play themselves into airy
extrusions of almost infinite length.
Cooler heads never prevail
but cling to whatever it was that made them.
Learned astronomers, looking up
from blackboards covered with dense equations
and long computer print-outs affirm
the big bang we've all lived through
and can't remember, although we know
that nothing was the same before
and nothing will ever undo it now
except by erasing what we are,
its creatures and its heirs. The eyes
close and we turn our attention inward,

deeper and deeper, digging for China,
gold, diamonds, the seething truth.
At that depth, in the heat and pressure,
magma leads a life of its own
and the firm earth trembles, twitches,
an animal dreaming life as it is.
Milton knew what Samson saw
and Oedipus discovered—darkness
in which ruin can fall away
as easily as joy. One learns
to stand still, the eyes closed,
breathing slowly, attending and then
not attending. The clumsy body
comes into its own and one
consults it, avoiding condescension,
avoiding envy, for we arrive
at the same end at the same time
and owe one another, for odd favors
exchanged at odd times, an honest
acceptance, and even some regard.

Jephthah's Prayer

We know, although we never pronounce,
the name of the Lord. But Jephthah's daughter?
Who was she? Her name appears
nowhere, as if her blood had blotted
out identity itself,
as if the Jews—and even Jehovah—
looking back, felt ashamed
that He was no better than Poseidon
who exacted from the king of Crete
the same terrible tribute, promised
the same sporty way: *Whatever*
I shall meet shall be the Lord's
(Who therefore shared in the choice of victim
and also the blame). Idomeneo
meets Idamante and everyone sings
his heart out until, at the end,
Poseidon relents and we're given to feel
relief that the barbarous age is over.
That was the message Abraham
and the young Isaac brought back from
Moriah's wilderness: the Jews
and their God ought not behave
like Aztecs. Still, at moments of stress,
we offer extravagant bargains, ruinous
deals that are never refused, as Jephthah
learned, whose eyes were opened only
the moment he saw his daughter's close:
the world is not a just world,
and God is not a righteous God.
Worship, stupid or insincere
as all of it is, can neither please
nor placate the blind and brutal power
creation everywhere demonstrates.
Innocence slaughtered, and no hand
raised to stop it, no voice
calling out in protest? Worship . . . ?
Jephthah, Israel's judge, discerned
the joke of it and in cold anger
kept his silence to let them believe,

and let them think he still believed:
Let them, like savages, recite
their old formulas and take
what fools' comfort they can. One day,
sooner or later, a time will come
when disaster will reveal to them
their folly, as all of them go, believing
in the prayers they still recite, to die
in thousands and in tens of thousands,
animals led off to be butchered,
for after the one, the rest are easy,
a schoolboy's copybook exercise
to prove how triangles or gods
behave. One must be long in patience
as the dead are patient until the day
when a furnace glare shall dye the skies
and God shall have His own back,
in his watering eyes and nostrils, the stench
of suffering innocence, His children,
mine but multiplied by millions,
for she was all, the equal of all
light and life. You can hear in the end
an echo of the beginning thunder
that what had been done might be undone,
as Jephthah thought but did not need
to pray aloud: Let there be darkness.

Old Photo

After years in a drawer with the film still in the camera,
its instants preserved in an Instamatic's belly,
it is not surprising that the prints come out skewed
to the rose we're taught to expect of memory, be
on guard against. The faces of my children
(when did Evan still wear those glasses, or Sarah
wear her hair that way?) help with the dating.
Mother looks the same. The Quinlans' tree
had not yet been cut down. Neither had Mother.
Josh clowns with a fallen branch from the oak
that still lords it over the yard. He thinks
that shirt was one he wore in the eighth grade.
If he's right, that was the last time all three
were there at the house together with Mother and Dad
who never were much for cameras—which explains
how this half-shot roll of film got left for six
or seven years. I took it to be developed
to see what moment of passage, what special occasion
had prompted a last session of holding still
and smiling into the sun: the children's visit
on an ordinary summer day. The Purdys'
flowers are all in bloom in rose and mauve.
Mother's face in the one shot is far away.
Dad doesn't even appear. I close my eyes
to see better, but not better enough.

Unveiling

Jeder Engel ist schrecklich.
—Rilke

Eddying winds, dust laden, busy themselves
in fitful domestic chores, polish
and tidy up, but over time grind down,
wearing the face of stone back to smoothness
as before the names got carved. Listen,
that sound the wind makes is that of the names
unsaying themselves in the grave mouths of the dead.
Among the living, too, gritty bits
of the world of matter that claims to matter
deface our clearest images. Details
relax their tenacious grip, run off
to hide in the barren landscape. Bereft
past grief to rage, we cannot think
how we could have let ourselves be cozened,
our losses so compounded. But it happens.
Vandals are merciless, and we share
in the blame, for those shy spirits
like all nocturnal creatures are easily startled,
and we are clumsy, noisy, and maladroit.
Worse, we prefer what is tidy and smooth.
Bad faith, bad taste, and fatigue conspire,
and pain saps our strength, even for this
impotent protest. Vulgar plaster saints
comfort, and the tintypes that grace our walls.
Forgivable lapses? Such violent forgetting
is no worse dishonor than what we do
throwing out old socks and underwear,
all those shoes, the ties no longer in fashion,
the vitamins and medicines, their cure
found at last. Harder to hold on to:
the imperfections on both sides, the impatience
on both sides, the thoughtlessness that marred
the tyrannous ideal we gave lip service
and to which we now promote them, doing them wrong
in a good cause, weeping, then dry-eyed
but no better able to see. The blindness
of young lust commends itself as charmed
and charming, or anyway necessary.

They settle on one another, persuading themselves
that he or she will do whatever it is
the script calls for as well as another.
Such indiscriminate longing turns
enemy in the end, its bad habits
of a lifetime the impediments and traducers
of love, which isn't clear and can't stand
still to look at what it claims to crave,
gaze fixedly at it, and then, eyes closed,
summon up the details of a face
worth all the world. The heads on Easter Island
are more expressive, better detailed. I forget
along with you, let go as I assume
that you are letting go: but then you pause,
turn back, reproachful, as vivid as ever.
Then, like Eurydice, you hesitate,
reconsider and disappear again.
These shocks, diminishing in intensity,
so exquisitely timed and calibrated,
welcome, precious, are not to be commanded.
For these ambiguous gifts, we learn to offer
our qualified thanks and admit that conventional prayers
for the spirit's repose are trickier than they seem,
pious impostures for—see—the eyes are open,
the cunning devil knows it's his own repose
he begs for, and at what cost:
that effortless glycerine tears should mark
the course that once his real tears tracked,
burning their way like lava. Fainter and fainter,
the artist pulls his engraving from the stone,
wearing the image smooth, as water or wind
will in time. The last loss is of loss,
the mind's failure, the heart's damnable health.

Parodos

Χο. καὶ μὴν ἐγώ σοι πένθος ὡς φίλος φίλῳ
λυπρὸν συνοίσω τῆσδε καὶ γὰρ ἀξία.
—*Alcestis* 369, 370

Whoever the hero, whatever his crime,
between the scenes of his agony, the chorus
comes to speak their nostrums for us,
to reassure, and yet at the same time,
in elevated Doric to suggest
what community at its best
can be and how our mere attendance is
a limit if not a cure for nemesis.

The formal pattern of their saying,
more than anything they say, assuages
the pain we feel, the hero's rages,
and the griefs that loom before us. The rhythm of praying,
even to gods who will not hear, is some
comfort. Neither stupid nor dumb,
they turn first one way, then the other, and then
stand, immobile, bearing what they can.

We all have had our catastrophes
at which we cried in demotic or simply wailed
beyond comfort. Belief failed,
and nothing in Aeschylus or Sophocles
helped except the chorus, who murmured, numerous,
inarticulate, very nearly humorous,
but nevertheless conveying with each word
what sheep bleat to each other in the herd.

The cold comfort they provide
is never adequate to the hero's loss,
but here they file in their parodos
with wisdom that seems somehow to have multiplied
by a sympathetic resonance that rings
response on any similar strings
of harp or heart that happen to be near,
much as in the transaction we call prayer.

But what the chorus says does not
imply much faith, as they stand there and wait
to see how the hero will meet his fate.

They're not blind, have seen, in fact, a lot,
and know what to expect, as well as we
for whom they speak—and from whom will be
chosen the next agonist, whose moan,
however dreadful, will not be alone.

It's the best bargain one can strike
or wring from the texts. I do not believe in heaven,
but still pray for six or seven
decent souls about me. I should like
comforters, mourners, sounds of human speech
around me. You, whom these words reach,
faute de mieux will do—for whom this verse
will stand as thanks or, if you fail me, curse.

Caution

There comes a time when you can bear no more,
some random scrap of news having proved to be
the straw that breaks your spirit's back. New York
has owls in every borough big enough
to take a good-sized cat? You feel their wings
beating the air over your head and resolve
    never to leave your house.

You recognize the rightness right away
of this avoidance of such pain and pity
as everywhere abound, but the sound of rubber
squealing on pavement, the silence, and then the smash
of glass and metal break into that tight circle
you've drawn. You draw it tighter, smaller, and promise
    never to go downstairs.

The feeling, nevertheless, persists of risk,
dreadful and universal. You don't quite trust
your mental status, but isn't that just another
proof, another worry? What can you do
but carry on somehow, as conquered countries
always have, and face it that you are likely
    never to leave your room.

With blankets drawn up to your neck, it should
be safe, but panic still takes your breath away.
Your heart races; you often break into the cold
sweats of the last judgment. The baseball bat
you keep within easy reach may be of some
use. There's no more retreat, now that you've sworn
    never to leave your bed.

Rat

The dog knew first, heard it or smelled it,
and rousing himself from his age, snuffled, went for it,
stalking ass-tight alert. And then we saw it,

a blur with a tail from behind the cutting board
to behind the stove. One of the youngsters screamed.
I grabbed a broom. The dog scratched at the wall,

bloodlust up, while I banged under the stove,
my stomach tight as the dog's ass, from anger
that our citadel was breached, our civility ripped

away, our decencies turned suddenly slum.
From under the stove, the broom drew hanks of dust.
—to prove we deserved such a visitation?—and sounds

of the rat moving. The dog barked. The rat
broke, ran through the door to the laundry room.
I closed that and opened the outside door

to the back yard to let it make its escape.
Afraid or stubborn, it wouldn't, but crouched behind
the door. I reached for whatever—a snow shovel

(clumsy weapon but better than nothing) and poked,
and he wriggled through underneath the hinge.
When he was halfway I slammed the door

closed. The high screak of ratpain pierced me;
I opened; he shrilled again but didn't move.
To dispatch him, I approached with the snow shovel

as if with a halberd. He saw it and wriggled through,
out, and away. To die, I suppose. I hope,
to die quickly. I went inside for a gin.

A week since, and the house has not quite healed;
kitchen and laundry room are still tender.
We try to go on with playing the play of our lives

with its set decorations and props of crystal and china,
speaking our lines as if we still believed them,
and hoping to forget the untoward event

that has shown it up as sham, turned it to farce.
Filthy luck, screams, death, the bad
smell: there's nothing to say. Where is the gin?

Wilson's Pen

Wilson's Pen Is Ready. Thus, the headline announced,
the treaty not yet signed, their man in Versailles
still standing by. Some editor said, "Go!"
unaware that the banner's second
line ran the middle words too close
together and to the truth.

The second edition was different, even though
Wilson went ahead and signed with whatever
instrument came to hand—a fountain pen
no doubt, but Europe was no less fucked
for that. Self-determination
is a game history plays

rougher than gentlemen imagine and always
for keeps. But the newsboys' hoarse laugh, prophetic
enough, rings in the air every morning
still, for other reasons, as I sit
down at my desk to take once more
that unreliable pen

in hand in an attempt to perform the great trick
that may not, of course, work: so I risk chagrin,
by now an old companion. The odds are
always long. Even the big Mont Blanc's
burly power is null without
the consent of the goddess

to whom, when it comes, one learns to give thanks,
    knowing
how much is her free gift and how little skill's
desert. (Can women poets understand,
holding a mute pen, a mere machine,
what the ritual figures and how
a bared nib quickens or dies

according to the occasion, the concord of
cue and sensibility, not to speak of
how long it's been since the last time? Are they
able to fake this too, whatever
their reasons? That assurance, we
sometimes envy but don't want.)

Our silences are what in the end give speech
its resonance, as the miles of barren sand
set an oasis, a jewel in that
dry shimmer. Would parched lips part to lie?
The pen, I say, has a will of its
own, will not be commanded,

and, as Wilson demonstrated, to pick it up
is to take our lives in our hands. The sword is
less mighty, even stuck into a stone
where it can say only *yes* or *no*.
This, though, can calibrate the soul,
measuring worth or its lack

with intimidating precision. It's said that
in primitive tribes, medicine men and chiefs
wear them, who cannot write a word. They know
magic wands when they see them and show
daring, as they would displaying
vipers asleep at their breasts.

Guts

All that fine-tuned high-toned discrimination,
where does it get you? Evaporating like foam
on the hard line of hot sand, it's cute
but has nothing to do with the depth or pressure of truth's

mucky bed. To feel in the guts is to claim
less but more, their crude fundamental reports
being of pain or not, distention or
relief, or the pleasant fullness of having dined

well. The head is a clever place but hardly
the domicile of the self, that big but shy
tube-within-a-tube, that deep-sea creature
of autonomic certainties you invoke

as too dumb to lie when something matters
enough for it to notice or care about.
Or let it be rather that lazy baby
you once were and still largely are,

with rage and content its only modes, brooking
no nonsense except its own. Words
always fail, don't they, and meaning, prior
and urgent, slithers away. That imperious being

is all you can trust—even when it comes
to the bad news. The five senses fool you,
but here is common sense, the sixth sense
you never like to speak of, even though

it keeps your manor going—or the chateau
where you play the lord while strains of music offer
genteel diversion; but you remain alert
to catch one of its slight but ominous rumbles.

Tambourine

You think of gypsies, kindergarten brats,
and the glassy-eyed bimbo, always the least
adept of the group that calls itself musicians.
What does she do but bang it on her butt?

Pop and hiss, those contrarieties,
caught as they are in the tambourine's eternal
hoop, squabble, their bass and treble demands
upon our flagging attention, stupid, vulgar.

And music condescends to this, or aspires:
Baron Ochs, however else he is gross,
recoups a little, doesn't he, of our hearts,
baring his own with that simple wistful waltz,

its shallow depths his right and limpid pool?
What we remember of all the refinement, nuance,
and complication simplifies to that,
and the tambourine is the virtuoso player

of simplification flirting with boredom. Guess
if she or it be instrument for the other
to play—for we are not so circumscribed
as she. Acknowledge the little frisson they make

together, elemental, accommodating,
even promiscuous (any tune will do),
or close your eyes as hers are closed and conjure
any face you will. Dumb as she is

she knows how it is, how she's put upon,
but doesn't seem to mind as she dishes out
lucidities prefabricated for these
healthy inarticulate creatures, the forms

of feeling, the right vessels for what wine
their lives' *cuvée* may provide. The best will age,
mellow, deepen, but keep that scintillant
character, the nerves' tambourine thrill,

abstract, impersonal, and yet expressive
of what they are. Fortune, good or ill,

will compose the score, filling out the staves—
which is why gypsies, children in rhythm bands,

and adolescents, careering into the future,
like so well what most of us just suffer.
They bang and jangle, playing, thoughtless, eager,
happy, blindly happy. That's the skill.

The Whippets

At the levee, you remember all those busy
supernumeraries filling the stage
to represent not just the luxury
of the Marschallin's life but also the heavy demands
wealth can make on time and energy, problems
that burden only a few in the Grand Tier.
The milliner, chef, hairdressers in their mistress's
service command attention; other lesser
figures—the scholar, tenor, and noisy orphans—
beg and take what they can get. (The pushy
gossips, denied, will be back in the second act
to nudge the plot along.) Meanwhile, the crowd,
picturesque, dresses the stage, and offers
the audience something to look at. See, in the back,
that vendor of animals. Sometimes he's given a caged
bird or maybe a monkey, or, on this occasion,
a couple of dogs for their touch of lively disorder
and also to balance the blocking. It makes for a nice
effect worth the minimal risk one runs
with animals on stage. Who doesn't have stories . . . ?
Of the horse in *Aida*—or was it *Fanciulla del West?*—
that heard applause for the tenor and, circus trained,
broke for the footlights to take its hard-learned bow.
Still, on a brace lead, a pair of whippets . . .
How can they fuck up?
                    The poor sod
stage director hadn't paid sufficient
attention to his libretto and its resigned
suggestion that our pretensions, or best intentions,
are doomed, even in love, or one might say
especially in love; and the pair of dogs
(as Frederica von Stade daintily put it)
"fell in love and got married," right there on stage
so that Dr. Bohm had to lay down his baton
and wait while the audience, on its feet, delighted,
cheered. Octavian stood there, appalled although
the Marschallin was hardly disturbed and the Baron,
touched by such a display of innocence,
affected to stare out through an upstage window

at the prospect of a garden the sly designer
had indicated there, a paradise
to which the busy whippets were harking back.
They made a trio Hofmannsthal and Strauss
might have liked but wouldn't ever have dared
write, too knowing in stagecraft and too shrewd
in love to take such chances (how does one get
dogs that will perform every night on cue?):

Octavian

Is that what it all comes down to, rapture or even
faithlessness, that simple animal act?
They are looking at dogs but what they see is me
an hour or so ago. I cannot endure
the shame of having been found out, but she
queens it along as if she weren't still
damp with me there. However does she do it?
We are supposed to be sovereign over the beasts
but the truth is that beastliness masters us.
The heart and other organs lunge, slip
from the leash and run wild, or drag us along
helpless. Ochs is inured to it, thinks it's funny,
and she'd agree except that she's unwilling
to admit to such indelicate amusement,
which may offer a hint of how she'll think
of me in a year's time. Or will I be
like him, a lecher and cynic, remembering her,
if I do at all, as another name on my list?
It's true, dreadful and true, which is why they laugh
out in the dark pit, watching us fall
—or have we already fallen?—to their level.

The Marschallin

That too, or that first and last,
but what we add transforms both it and us
to another realm, refined and elevated,
as the power of speech can turn a simple fear
or desire into articulated thought.

Civilization admits, or even depends,
on nature's crude *données* but, as at table,
we try to carry on with a little grace.
Tearing into their meat, would they offend
Octavian's tender sensibilities so?
And I wonder, is it on my account or his own
that he's distressed? Supposing the latter, Ochs
pretends to stare out of the window displaying
a delicacy I shouldn't find so surprising,
for I, too, maintain a certain posture
as in a *tableau vivant*, and feel the strain
increase with time. We must endure the applause
as if it were what we deserved for this *coup de theatre*.

The Baron

Somewhere beyond shame, there's a shamelessness
for which we dig deep in the mud, a twin
of innocence. Those whippets, rutting away
onstage, are purer than music that hung in the air
like mathematics' body. We're old dogs,
my friends out there applauding and I, schoolchildren
again, staring out in the yard to study
the lesson a couple of strays taught, going at it
a dog's age ago. Where are those children?
What has time done to us? Or ask
how else to defy time except with that
repetitive stratagem? The joke is old
but still good for a smile if it's well told,
which is why they applaud. But see how the youngster
    blushes.
I would not change places, be young again
and run such risks—to be obliged to repeat
those strenuous exercises by which the soul
becomes at last limber even while the body
weakens and swells to what you see.
                                    They're done?
Yes, and the maestro raises his baton
for us to resume the pursuit of our quarry of meaning,

driven, perhaps hounded, but not forgetful
of who we are or where we are in the score.

*

They settle down and return to the transaction
of the opera's business. Once again, the Baron
will pay and depart and, with somewhat better grace,
the Marschallin will exit, leaving the stage
to the young lovers, as she has to do in production
after production. The cast, timbres, tempi
and lighting vary some, but the action is always
exactly the same. Next time, darlings, the parrot
(one that never talks) or maybe the monkey
(but prepubescent, and wearing little trousers) . . .
Whatever "life" the scene may require we can
manage to indicate for intelligent people
who understand well enough the risks of love.

Mocking Bird

So let them come, white coated, their tape recorders
set to catch the notes of various species
of birds, each of them performing—encore! encore!—
the one trick he knows.

To sing the self is anybody's business,
but the mockingbird goes beyond to try on other
possible lines and lives, mimic, improve,
improvise upon,

and imagine creations in which the flights of birds
and their fancies are truly free in a way those
dodoes in lab coats could never dream, much less
get down to analyze

for a learned paper. Their playback buttons always
produce sameness which isn't at all the same
as what the mockingbird would do, playing
(for that's what it is).

The territorial claims and mating calls
the other birds warble are propaganda.
Art should be *inutile*; mundane concerns
of living elicit

meaner modes in him. Should another mock-
ingbird intrude on his private space, he'll squawk,
threaten violence, though birds of other kinds
he tolerates as themes

for his variations, occasions. Even humans—
at our best, that is—can arrest his interest,
with a radio, say, at a picnic, playing a sax
riff (of Charlie Bird?)

that he may pick up and even jam with a little
before letting it go, as the moment passes
(always before we are ready) and he moves on
the gift of his noting.

Reading

The hour or so before any poetry reading
I spend at my desk at home, or more than likely
sprawled on a motel bed, flipping my old
pages . . . they're an album of my life.
Honest, I can admit to recognizing
here and there something stirring that stirred
before. Mostly, I'm heartless and can't imagine
what of these old loves once drew me to them
or what we thought we had together. The reader,
who may in theory exist, is faithful as I'm
not, may take to his heart one of these dim
darlings, settle down with her, be happy
ever after, habit filling the rents
in meaning or grace that trouble me now. Picky,
picky . . . yes. And faithless, a pudgy Don
Juan on the prowl. My clever tongue, my seducer's
eye have served me long but turn against me.
It's a conceit, of course, but something's true.
Will I tell them to keep their women close, to love them
better than I've loved mine? And if I do
will they know it's for the sport, to make the game
tougher and more fun? They expect their poets
to behave badly. How shall I disappoint them?
A quick nip from the flask will get me through this,
but sooner or later the liver rebels, and the life.

Excursion to Pergamon

Ruins and the simple life—for these,
we will pay much, suffer much. The nozzles
overhead in the coach produce no whisper
of cool air, while outside on the steep
slope, women in black lug bundles of sticks
to camels under a tree. An odd system,
but what we have come to see as much as the *castro*
on top of the mountain. The holy places now
are any that speak to us, however crudely,
of what we have lost (or deferred, we tell ourselves)
and how we have wasted our energies.
                                    Look at these stones,
every one hewn smooth and hauled up here
to make a wall that was breached anyway—all
walls must be—so that Alexander's treasure
is gone. And still we knock ourselves out for our
trifle. We imagine life here, try
the wine, risk the water, acquire the score
or fifty words one needs to get by with, learn
the main streets of the town, and are not even startled
at a turn in the road to confront in a shop window
faces that under the unfamiliar hats
turn out to be our own. The rate of exchange
varies from day to day, and one can always
haggle some for sport, but the hard bargains
are those we drive with ourselves while the motorscooters
whine or snarl all night beneath our window.
Can we visit shrines, acknowledge their truth, and return
the way we came, as if the colonnades
were still upright, the arches still intact,
and not one book overdue from one of the world's
trio of great libraries, that hole
we looked down into from the excavation's
lip? Achievement comes to this. Ambition
or mere boredom drives the best away
from the tiresome pieties life in a pretty village
depends on (and the same reliable jokes)
to Athens, Paris, London, Rome, or New York—
where these people vacation. Or Africa,

for a two-week tour of the iron age. Ridicule
works for a while (anything works for a while)
to keep the large shaggy beast at bay;
it returns nevertheless like one of those hungry
cats that prowl the tavernas and have staked out
a table or two at the station of some cross
waiter. We try the village version of grappa,
strong, raisiny, crude. I do not allude
to these dark thoughts, unseemly for a vacation,
but point instead to the white goat that grazes
a patch of wasteland behind us. All day long
the sun has beaten down on that dry hill,
but the goat has found a patch of shade near a scrub
bush (or is it a half-dead tree?). It can't
last. Someone will come, charcoal maker
hefting his ax, or butcher with his knife,
or the sun will simply relent and set. Let's hope.
With the local *eau de vie* we drink to life—
it's raw, almost bitter, but then it's cheap.

Amphion's Lyre

We know the dangers. Think of the trumpets
before Jericho's walls, the blast
that somehow brought them tumbling down—
a problem of physics more than belief,
for we've all seen the commercials, a singer's
high note, live or on tape,
and the shattering glass, and none of us questions
how it can happen or doubts his eyes.
Such excess is more than likely
to disturb the calibrations by which
we've learned to live. Whatever walls
there are will probably shudder, shatter
to rubble. Plato warned us against
poets, musicians, dangerous people
with no idea of their own power,
where it comes from or how to use it.
The case is worse than Plato imagined,
unfamiliar with Japanese
customs and folkways. Wandering *ronin*
studied the flute, the *shakuhachi*,
an instrument demanding control
of the breathing muscles, and therefore training,
but also a way of making a living,
for the repertoire of the flute included
conventional pieces for passing the hat:
unemployed, the *ronin* still
needed to eat. There were also selections
for meditation, simulacra
of wind in the pines or running water,
not so different from our own music
in echoing nature. But the *shakuhachi*,
one and two-thirds feet in length,
was also a bludgeon, a billy club
they learned to use, not a concealed
but disguised weapon that could be deadly.
Civic arenas sell out in hours
now for punk-rock performers: kids
flock to the theater of cruelty, high

on the keening notes of electric pain
that have always lain there among the frets
waiting for idle fingers to find
and pluck them out. We connoisseurs
know where to look: in library stacks,
they lie in wait in the cool dark,
just as paintings on gallery walls
keep their counsel until the guards
turn away, and then will riot,
beckon, and mock tycoons and elders
who think they own them. Rebels, rabble,
or worse, brats, they make rude noises
breeding teaches us how to ignore
or even forget. Who would give children
hallucinogens and stimulants
as strong as these? What can they learn
but passion, excess, and, even worse,
dissatisfaction that's sure to grow,
making the lives they're likely to lead
insupportable, turning decent
if dull pleasures into occasions
for self-reproach. What kind of present
is that to give a youngster? Or ask
yourself what painting, music, dance,
or poetry ever built. The question,
loaded, is what the uncultivated
have learned to throw in our faces, a lunk
uncle or smart-ass brother-in-law
letting it slip sooner or later.
There aren't many ready answers
that spring to mind; and only later,
after the anger has burnt away,
one may perhaps remember the story
of how Amphion played on the lyre
music of so rare a strain
that the rocks flocked to hear it, climbed
one on another, so that the walls
of Thebes sprang thus into being—

a miracle answering and outdoing
that of the trumpets of Jericho.

2

Twins, infants, left on the mountainside . . .
You know what follows, not just from the many
stories of this kind you have read before,
but from the gut. A truth calls out, faint
but insistent as the infant voices squalling
from under the bushes. We're all left exposed
on perilous ground to take our chances. We all
deserved richer, safer, better, but hard
earth and the odds between wild beasts and kind
shepherds seems familiar. And the twins?
You recognize them too, embodiments
of ambivalence, of double natures, self
and what the self denies, or aspires to,
or fears but still learns to live with. Amphion
and Zetus then, were twins, left on Cithaeron,
found and reared to manhood and other chances.
The shepherd—perhaps it was his dog, first—heard them
and there were dismay and delight mixed, and wonder
at how life is and how some of us bear it.
There were also practical questions: who were the babies,
how had they come there, and for what dread fate
had they been destined? The shepherd picked them up,
afraid—let's give him that. Is he doing right?
Will this turn out in the end to be a kindness
or not? But he's no god, can't see that far
ahead. He has no choice and takes them home—
and that, we may suppose, is what their father
wanted all along; what Zeus assents to
happens, without any choice, that way.

3

Ignorance first, but then, with the passage of time,
something puzzles, something that will not fit
but binds them together. Their curiosity turns
into a shared obsession.

38

At last, the truth, or part of it, is revealed—
they're not the shepherd's flesh and blood but were left by
someone else to be found or to die—and they hate
whoever it was who did that.

Even their own mother? But what do they owe her?
They try to imagine her: selfish adultress or whore.
It makes no difference. They have each other now
and a vow to be revenged.

Their quest; adventures. They find her at last, that mother
whose breasts caked dry while for all she knew
they were starving or mauled to death on the mountainside
where she'd left them and walked away.

They hear Antiope's story . . . And now we are truly
suckered, as they were. The single purpose
blurs. There's always another side to the question.
Pity wells up in their eyes.

The twins hear what we've known all along,
that legacies of suffering can unite
as surely as blood. She has been seduced,
abandoned, kidnapped, rescued . . .

And that was just the beginning. She was married,
then spurned, put into prison, tortured,
was given up for dead, but she endured it
and somehow at last escaped.

She has been looking for them, searching herself
against all odds for the children of that first
passion, for Amphion and Zetus, twins
she bore to the great Zeus.

But who is not a demigod, or who
would deny that special providence, his own
rightful heritage? Destiny intervenes,
whenever, wherever it will,

to make us equal—parents and children; wives,
husbands, and lovers; rich and poor; the great
movers and shakers and any shepherd's children.
It's capricious, perhaps, but fair.

They join forces, the mother and her two
sons, all of them victims and vessels of fate
with nothing more to lose, resolved on vengeance,
instruments of the gods.

4

Guardian, uncle, husband, king,
    and also betrayer,
Lycus was all those things together,
    the man she had trusted,
had loved and then had learned to hate,
    whose death she envisioned—
the vision was all that kept her alive:
    Lycus and Dirce.
As a dog returns to re-eat his vomit,
    a married man
goes back to his old wife for a last
    good-bye fuck;
caught there in his old muck, he
    loves it and stays.
Both of them, then, the man and the woman,
    but one at a time,
and let their dying be long, painful,
    and disgusting enough
to hold her attention each lovely moment.
    That's what she asks for,
and that is what Amphion and Zetus
    promise to give her,
happy to find such justification
    for what they've both wanted
and now can make a proper claim to.
    Step-father, great-uncle,
Lycus is King of Thebes, whose throne
    the brothers will share.
Assassinations on such a scale are
    civil wars:
the fact that advantage attaches can always
    be denied.
So they have it both ways and can claim
    as destiny's children

to be acting blindly, only obeying
the sternest dictates
of implacable gods—though both the brothers
have probably peeked.
An opportunistic thought that crosses
the mind of one
occurs to the other right away.
Twins are like that.
Only Antiope's eyes are open,
but she sees nothing,
having already suffered enough
to have gone quite mad.

5

Antiope's story is muddled; different reports
stress now one, now another aspect
of the union of god with a virgin—a nasty business,

defying all the decencies: the bitch
staked out on the ice where the wolves will find her
and either kill her or mate with her. It's cruel

but a way to keep the sled dogs' bloodline strong.
And so, with us. But imagine Neanderthals,
a tribe of them, to whom one of us appears

to screw their daughters. It's a kind of promotion, really,
a chance for survival—and yet they are not grateful.
Resenting us, they disapprove of the girls

as if they'd cooperated, or even enjoyed it.
But what can one expect from Neanderthals?
Antiope, a king's daughter, must suffer

and the babies have to be separated from her
and put in some rustic setting so they can emerge
on their own merits later on. The shepherd's

hut is not very different from, say, a manger.
The humble raise themselves. The mighty fall.
For Antiope from there on it was pure

shit—Mary and Mary Magdalene
at the same time. There is a logic to it
that ought to produce twins. And also madness.

6

As a monster, Lycus
lacked imagination,
That is not surprising:
        torture doesn't need
any special talent
beyond the gift of dullness
that never wonders what it
        must feel like to bleed.

You see your chance and take it,
as he did when his brother,
Nycteus, the Theban
        king, began a war
over the kidnapping
of Antiope, his daughter,
who hardly was a Helen
        but just as much a whore.

What Epopeus, king of
Thessaly, had seen in
Antiope was hard for
        anyone to tell—
not that it much matters.
Nycteus was killed in
a fairly hard-fought battle,
        and Epopeus as well.

So Lycus took command and
returned to Thebes in triumph,
Antiope beside him.
        The air was filled with cheers.
And then he thought of marriage:
instead of being regent,
he'd be a king and bridegroom.
        "Live a thousand years!"

That's what everybody
in the agora shouted,
except perhaps for Dirce,
        the wife he'd put aside
in order to improve his
claim to rule the city.
He also bribed the army
        which drank to groom and bride.

Labdacus, the infant,
Nycteus' grandson,
the only other claimant
        to the throne was spirited
away before the thugs that
Lycus sent to kill him
got there—but no matter,
        if people thought him dead.

Lycus threw a party,
partly coronation,
partly celebration
        of the nuptual rite.
All of Thebes attended,
some in terror not to,
but most came for the scandal
        (it wasn't incest, quite,

but an uncle and a niece?) Now,
it's hardly every day that
a thing like that will happen.
        One didn't need a seer
to whisper the prediction
that nothing good would come of
such a match, or give it
        maybe half a year.

Rather less was needed
before the trouble started.
Lycus disappeared for
        hours every night.
Antiope complained, but

he gave no explanations.
Her tears did not affect him.
     He wouldn't even fight.

And then, out of the blue, there
came a brief announcement:
Antiope was ill and
     had to stay in bed.
Optimists believed it
might be true, for Lycus
would at least feign sorrow
     if the girl were dead.

Realists replied that
it wasn't very likely
he'd even make the effort;
     the realists, of course,
were right about that. Quickly,
Lycus sent for Dirce
as if they hadn't ever
     gone through a divorce.

Pessimists required
some time to imagine
something even worse than
     what everyone could see,
but soon their rumors started—
Lycus hadn't killed her;
somewhere in the dungeons,
     still, Antiope

was kept alive, was tortured,
and Dirce came to see her,
to watch her on the rack and
     listen to her screams.
But very few believed that
Thebes was taken over
and the world was being run by
     figments from bad dreams.

The pessimists turned out at
last to be correct and

Thebans were disgusted
      decades later, when
Antiope appeared to
confirm their worst suspicions.
They shook their heads together
      and swore: Never again!

7

Lycus is almost plausible, explains
he didn't do anything wrong—even believes
(or seems to) what he's saying. He could have killed
Labdacus, the baby, the heir, and didn't.
He could have killed Antiope and he didn't.
He just put her away—because he had to.
She'd gone mad. Jealousy had done it.
He admits his infidelity, but he explains it,
a man of the world speaking to men of the world,
as part of the job of ruling. The marriage had been
political—he never lied about that.
Antiope ought to have understood. A princess?
What had she expected? What had any
sensible person in Thebes supposed? The torture?
He swears he never had any part of that.
It was all Dirce's doing. He regrets it
and takes exception to the very nasty suggestion
that he connived with Dirce, or just to please her
kept poor crazy Antiope
alive as a kind of plaything. It just isn't so.
It's monstrous. He had no idea whatever
what was going on . . .
                    And Zetus, bored,
signals that the trial is over and finds
Lycus guilty. He smashes the man's skull
over and over until its pale pink goo
has covered the jagged rock he holds in his hand.

8

The other appeared to be easy,
beyond any possible question

after Antiope told them,
herself, how she had suffered,
the tortures she'd undergone—
and Dirce didn't deny it.
Zetus could let his brother
appear to share in their power.
A simple execution
is not a great challenge, even
for poets. What could he do?
How could he screw it up?
Vague, yes, inefficient,
not very good with detail,
not punctual, not
a reliable management type,
all that Amphion needed
to do was to give the order
and stand there and watch. But remember,
their mother, Antiope, wasn't
at all right in the head.
She wanted to draw it out
as much as possible, cruel
to answer back for cruel.
To this Amphion consented,
even to her suggestion
that Dirce be tied to a bull
and dragged to death on the rocks
in the fields outside the city.
Zetus, who would have resisted,
was rather surprised at his brother,
so fastidious always,
for having given consent.
It wasn't that Zetus objected
to the grisly business itself—
being stoned to death
wasn't so very uncommon,
and this just turned the victim
into a more active partner
to make it a livelier show.
Still, you'd expect a poet,

having imagination—
one would suppose it his forte—
might have been better prepared
for what he was going to see.
It didn't seem to affect
Antiope much, one way
or the other; she just stared.
But it hit Amphion hard,
watching the woman bounce,
bleed, cry out, quiet,
and after a while ooze,
leaving a shiny trail
as a slug does in a garden,
but red. And he had to stand there,
unblinking, enduring it all,
as if he were being punished.
That's what he told Zetus,
who replied with affectionate oaths.
But that was the first warning.
The machinery'd started to work.
Inspiration? It's rather
more like an irritation
to which the unconscious finger
keeps returning to scratch.
That image kept coming back,
and Amphion had to discover
a way to cope with it, manage
to set it off at a distance
or encapsulate it as art.
Whatever his private reason
(need or merely the habit),
he turned it into a poem,
the result of which was to wreck
that nice balance between them
Zetus had tried to arrange.
Lycus' dying was nothing,
a mere prelude to the story
of Dirce done to death
and then turning into a fountain . . .

whatever the hell that means.
In fact, a month or so later,
in a field a mile away,
some shepherd discovered a spring,
most probably an old one
that the run-off of recent rains
had revived. There was no connection
except what Amphion's poem
imposed. But it made him famous.
He had become the avenger
of all of his mother's wrongs.
Zetus now had to wonder
what his brother intended,
and whether for all those years
Amphion hadn't contrived
to hide a streak of meanness
along with some managerial
shrewdness. Or could it all be
dumb luck? Could there be so
much luck in the world?
Either way, he resolved
that it would not happen again.

9

A Song of Amphion

"What we yell in its stupid face
will not by even a whit deter it,
but how can we not yell?

I am going to die, you are going to,
and he, and she, and probably it will die.
There is nothing else to throw into the great chasm

widening moment by moment at our feet
but what we have made. It won't do any good,
but some of us may believe, and the rest feel better

for having tried, for having at least soothed
in the moment of agony our own torment's twin.
There is also always the chance that he, in his faith,

is right, and I, in my unbelief, am wrong,
too cautious, too timid, lacking in the real imagination
in which there is said to be tranquillity

and a peace I can almost imagine that I imagine."

10

Zetus built the wall; Amphion played his lyre—
    as simple as that. Anyone who was there
can tell you Zetus planned it, supervised the masons,
    even worked beside them himself, sighting
the hewn stones along the taut strings and plumb lines.
    His brother, worse then useless, was only a nuisance
good manners contrived to overlook. But the story
    is still told—how the walls around the city
of Thebes somehow sprang up, grew together, built
    themselves, because of the music Amphion played.
To call it magic is not to dismiss it as arrant nonsense.
    Miracles happen. Mysteries aren't mere
demonstrations of how we need more information.
    Stones came dancing together, embraced one another,
and froze, startled—why not? Because his brother
    would almost surely have killed him then and there—
which is not what the story tells us. So figure the other way,
    bet with the odds, and suppose that Zetus built it.
The legend at least suggests what the people of Thebes wanted
    and would have preferred. Take it as more than likely
that Zetus grabbed more than half the governing power,
    that his rule was harsh, was cruel enough to arouse
hatred first, then hopelessness, and the feeble fancies
    those who are desperate will sometimes invent for
        themselves,
not so much for escape as the momentary distraction,
    the instant's respite such daydreams can offer.
Zetus may have heard the stories going around,
    and for a while there was nothing he could do.
On state occasions the two brothers, the joint rulers,
    made their appearance together—at least for a while.
And then? It was only Zetus. Amphion was unable,
    regrettably, regretfully, to appear.

You're not surprised, are you? Musicians, poets, artists,
    tend to get edged out in the best of times.
Amphion disappeared, was locked away in the same
    dungeons his poor mother had once been locked in.
That was one of the rumors—and none of the others was
    cheerful.
        Oddly enough, the story about the wall
hung on, clung to the wall like a sprig of ivy,
        digging itself in, delicate, fragile,
but tough as the stone itself once it has taken hold.

11

When the world turns nasty, we turn away
to others, better or simpler, that we invent
in dreams or art,
and what we flee prefigures what we yearn for.
Zetus, Amphion's twin, had imagination,
which is dangerous with power. He could
think up new orders to impose,
new laws or no laws.
Let us say mannerism in politics
is tyranny by a politer name.
But Amphion, no innocent either,
idly plucking the strings of his instrument,
played upon men's hearts a politician's aria
they knew to fear. Feeling the damage start,
they read the pages of their own souls' banned books.

Each looked to the ages, eager to daub
eternity's blank canvas and make upon it
his individual mark.
What they inflicted and what they suffered,
how they arrived at that satiety we dread
and envy, where it seems perhaps a gift
after all to be mortal,
wanting not another breath of time . . .
From such hints do we read the lives
of saints and monsters.

Amphion simply disappeared.
Zetus ruled for years, neither better nor worse
than any other king, and then, abruptly
died—either from sickness
or poison, the gods' displeasure or man's.
Anyway, he died, and with no issue.
Runners went out in the four directions
to find Labdacus, grandson of Nycteus,
that infant heir who had fled many years before.
When Labdacus died on the way back to Thebes,
his son, Laius, inherited, carrying on the line:
he married Jocasta. Oedipus was their son.